Broke to Business Boss

Money's Not the Problem.
Mindset Is

By

Eric F Gilbert

ISBN: 978-1-968365-08-0

About the Author

Eric F. Gilbert:

The Hustler With Hooks, Heart, and Heat

From shrimp boats to stock charts, Eric's the kind of guy who can land a 180-lb tarpon *and* a 7-figure turnaround, and drop a trading tip that hits 70% return before lunch. A lifelong Tampa Bay area fisherman turned serial entrepreneur, Eric blends salty know-how with business smarts.

As founder and president of VizzyBrand Marketing, he's spent decades helping businesses grow through public speaking, bold branding, and high-converting event marketing. He's led turnarounds, engineered exits, and built brands from the ground up. He's led struggling businesses to profitable exits through precise marketing and sales alignment.

He also runs **GetStockTips.com**, where traders tap into his no-nonsense daily picks — not financial advice, just tips that make money. Fast, focused, and high-performing.

Whether he's scaling up a brand or casting into skinny water at sunrise, Eric doesn't just play the game. He rewrites the rules.

Table of Contents

Chapter 5: The $0 Startup Toolkit

Free Tools to Launch, Manage, and Grow Your Business

Chapter 6: Legal and Legit for Less

How to Start a Real Business Without Getting Ripped Off

Chapter 7: Building a Brand That Sticks

Logos, Names, and Online Presence on a Budget

Chapter 8: Getting Clients Without Ads

Proven Guerrilla Marketing Tactics

Chapter 9: Using Social Media to Look Bigger Than You Are

How to Appear Professional and Scale Trust

Chapter 10: Growing Fast Without Funding

Using Cash Flow and Creativity to Scale

Introduction:

You Don't Need Money, You Need a Mindset

The truth is this: your bank account doesn't define your future. Your thoughts do.

There's a reason thousands of people with nothing have built powerful businesses from the ground up, while others with all the resources in the world never move an inch. It's not luck. It's not timing. It's not who you know. It's what you believe—and how consistently you act on those beliefs.

Think and Grow Rich taught us that wealth starts in the mind. **The Secret** reminded us that we attract what we expect. **The Slight Edge** showed that it's the little things, done daily, that change everything. This book brings all of that together—and strips away the fluff.

You're about to learn how to build a real business, not with a fat stack of cash, but with grit, clarity, and daily action. No loans. No investors. No excuses. Just hustle, knowledge, and smart decisions made one day at a time.

Every chapter in this book gives you practical tools. You'll learn how to start with zero dollars and still build something profitable. You'll learn how to market without spending a dime. You'll find out how to register your business legally for less than what most gurus charge for a webinar.

But first, you must believe that it's possible.

Because it is.

Warren Buffett—the Oracle of Omaha—didn't come from money. He started by delivering newspapers, collecting bottle caps, and reinvesting tiny profits as a child. He bought his first stock at 11 years old. He didn't start with millions—he started with a mindset. A belief that compound action, compounded over time, leads to wealth beyond imagination. That belief, paired with consistent effort and smart decisions, made him one of the richest men alive.

So if you're broke right now, consider yourself in good company. Some of the greatest fortunes in the world were built from empty pockets and strong convictions.

You'll hear real examples. You'll use real tools. You'll follow a path that's worked not just once, but repeatedly. You won't just read about becoming a boss—you'll become one, step by step.

Your transformation doesn't start with money. It starts with a decision. The moment you choose to stop living paycheck to paycheck, to stop doubting yourself, and to stop waiting for permission—that's when everything shifts.

And if you follow through, it won't be long before people stop asking what you do for a living and start asking how you did it.

Let's begin.

Chapter 1: Broke Isn't Broken

Being broke isn't a dead end. It's a starting line.

Most people think they need money to make money. But that's not how real wealth is built. Money follows value—and value comes from vision, grit, and execution. Being broke strips away your distractions and exposes your drive. It sharpens your focus because you don't have the luxury of wasting time.

The truth is, when your back is against the wall, you become resourceful. You make calls you wouldn't normally make. You take risks you'd usually avoid. You hustle harder because there's no safety net.

That pressure? It's not your enemy. It's your fuel.

In fact, some of the most iconic entrepreneurs started with less than you. Oprah Winfrey was raised in poverty. Daymond John started selling shirts from his mother's house. Steve Harvey slept in his car for years while chasing his dream. What they had in common wasn't money—it was relentless belief and daily action.

This chapter is about reframing how you see your current situation. Broke is temporary. Broke is common. But staying broke—that's a decision.

Here's what you have right now that money can't buy:

Time (which you can trade for value)

Creativity (which costs nothing but pays everything)

Access to free tools and platforms (the internet is your warehouse, your ad agency, and your megaphone)

Freedom to try, fail, and pivot (you're not protecting a big investment—you're free to experiment)

If you start seeing your lack of money as an opportunity to build smarter, leaner, and faster, you'll already be ahead of most people.

Some of the world's greatest business minds got their start from nothing—or lost everything and had to start again.

Take Dave Sandler, the founder of Sandler Sales. He developed a world-famous sales system that's still used today, but it didn't start in a high-rise office. In fact, when he was completely broke, he would intentionally drive to meetings with no money in his pocket. Then he'd park in paid parking lots where he couldn't leave unless he paid the fee. That meant he had to close a deal that day. Not only that, he had to ask for payment upfront and in cash, or he'd have no way to get his car out of the lot and go home. That kind of pressure created a level of focus and commitment most people never reach. And it worked. He built a multimillion-dollar training empire from that exact mindset.

Robert Kiyosaki, the author of "Rich Dad Poor Dad," also hit rock bottom. Long before the book made him a household name, Kiyosaki had made a fortune in education and investments—and then lost everything. He ended up sleeping in his car, broke and humiliated. But he didn't let it define him. He applied the same principles he taught others—principles of financial literacy, leverage, and business systems—to rebuild from scratch. That's what separates someone who's "rich once" from someone who can build wealth again and again. It's not luck. It's mental software. It's strategy, execution, and belief.

Howard Schultz, the man behind Starbucks, grew up in public housing in Brooklyn. His father worked low-paying jobs without benefits, and the family often struggled. Schultz saw firsthand what it meant to be broke. When he joined Starbucks, it was just a small local coffee roaster. He envisioned something bigger—coffee shops that felt like a community space. Investors told him it would never work. But Schultz persisted. He borrowed against everything he had, scraped together resources, and built what is now a global brand. From the projects to billions—that's the power of vision plus execution.

Warren Buffett—the Oracle of Omaha— didn't come from wealth. He was born in the middle of the Great Depression and started building his fortune as a child. At just six years old, he bought six-packs of Coca-Cola and sold each bottle individually at a profit. By the age of 11, he purchased his first stock. He reinvested every penny, flipping small profits into bigger ones. Buffett didn't inherit millions—he compounded small wins over decades. His early grind, resourcefulness, and long-term mindset are exactly what made him a billionaire. And he's not the exception—he's proof that consistent effort, patience, and strategic thinking pay off over time.

These examples aren't just meant to inspire you. They're meant to prove a point: wealth doesn't start with money.

It starts with:

A refusal to accept your current situation as permanent

A belief that you're capable of more

A commitment to learn what you don't know

A daily grind that compounds over time

You already have access to the most important tools:

Time — and how you use it will determine everything

Information — with the internet, there's no excuse for ignorance

Free platforms and tools — to build, promote, and deliver value

Urgency — because unlike people with money, you don't have the option to procrastinate

If you treat "broke" like a launchpad instead of a label, you'll gain something that can never be taken from you: ownership of your life.

This book will show you how. You don't need a loan, an investor, or a partner to get started.

You need purpose.

You need persistence.

You need a plan—and you're holding it in your hands.

Now let's turn your pressure into power.

Let's get to work.

Chapter 2: Mindset Makeover

If you want to run a business, you need to think like a business owner. And that means eliminating the excuses, the fear, and the self-doubt that's been holding you back.

You don't need more motivation. You need more discipline.

You don't need a miracle. You need a routine.

And most importantly—you don't need permission. You need a decision.

Let's start here: What you think determines what you do. And what you do determines what you get.

This is what separates the successful from the struggling. The average person thinks in terms of limitations:

"I don't have enough money."

"I don't have experience."

"What if I fail?"

A business boss thinks in terms of possibilities:

"How can I turn this into something profitable?"

"Who can help me figure this out?"

"What's the smallest step I can take today to move forward?"

That shift is everything.

Your Mindset Is Your Operating System

Think of your mindset like the software that runs your business. If you've got bugs—fear, procrastination, negative beliefs—you'll crash every time the pressure hits.

To reprogram your mind, you've got to become intentional about what you allow in. Your inputs determine your outputs. If you constantly surround yourself with broke mindsets, toxic social media, and excuses, don't be surprised when you start believing the same garbage.

Start replacing that input with new code:

Books from entrepreneurs who started with nothing

Podcasts from people who've built real businesses

Daily reminders of what you're building and why

This isn't just feel-good fluff. Neuroscience backs it up. Studies show that the brain can physically rewire itself based on repetition and belief—a concept known as neuroplasticity. That means if you consistently feed your brain new thoughts and reinforce them through action, your default behavior will start to change. You'll become someone who takes action instead of stalling. Someone who finds solutions instead of problems.

Identity Drives Behavior

People don't do what they want—they do what fits their identity. If you still see yourself as "just someone with an idea," you'll never move. But if you begin to see yourself as a business owner— before the revenue, before the LLC, before the first sale—you'll begin acting like one.

That means:

Showing up every day to work on your hustle

Learning what you don't know

Making moves that feel uncomfortable

Case Study: Sara Blakely, founder of Spanx, was selling fax machines door-to-door when she got her billion-dollar idea. She didn't wait until she had a factory or a business plan. She saw herself as the CEO before anyone else did. And she acted like it. That identity drove her through rejection after rejection until she made it.

Replace "Can't" With "How"

A powerful exercise for any entrepreneur is to start replacing the word can't with how. Instead of saying "I can't start without money," ask "How can I start without money?"

This single change in language forces your brain to seek solutions instead of shutting down. It turns dead ends into doorways.

Example:

"I can't afford a website." becomes "How can I create a free site with what I have now?"

"I can't run ads." becomes "How can I market without spending money?"

"I can't find clients." becomes "How can I reach people for free today?"

The Slight Edge Principle

Jeff Olson's The Slight Edge introduced a powerful concept: Simple things, done daily, compound into success.

Reading one page a day adds up to 365 pages in a year.

Making one sales call per day adds up to 365 potential clients.

Improving 1% each day makes you 37x better in one year (backed by math: $1.01^{365} \approx 37.8$).

This isn't about grinding until burnout. It's about consistency. The people who win long-term aren't usually the fastest or the flashiest. They're the ones who just didn't quit.

Your Environment Is Your Reality

The people you hang out with, the content you consume, and the habits you reinforce are shaping your business right now—whether you realize it or not.

Ask yourself:

Are the people around me building me up or holding me back?

Is my time spent on creation or consumption?

What am I reinforcing daily—action or avoidance?

Action Plan:

1. Create a daily mindset routine (5–10 min per day)

2. Write a new identity statement: "I am a business owner building [your idea] from the ground up."

3. Practice the "how" question every time you hit a wall

4. Track small wins daily to build momentum

5. Clean up your environment—online and offline

This chapter isn't the hype section. It's the hard truth: **your business will only grow as fast as your mindset does.**

You're not waiting to become someone new.

You're remembering who you were before the fear set in.

Let's keep moving. Your next move? Finding your hustle.

Chapter 3: Finding Your Hustle

You don't need to reinvent the wheel. You just need to find the right set of wheels to ride.

This chapter is about helping you identify a profitable hustle—something you can start with little or no money, that aligns with your skills, interests, or experience.

The Truth About Hustles

A hustle isn't just a job. It's a gateway. It's a bridge between where you are and where you're trying to go. Unlike a traditional business that may take years to build, a hustle is something you can launch in days—not months.

In a world where over 60 million Americans now work freelance (Statista, 2023), the idea of the side hustle isn't optional anymore—it's normal. And in many cases, it's the testing ground for a full-scale business.

But not all hustles are created equal. Some take forever to gain traction. Others burn you out before they pay off. Your job is to pick a hustle that's lean, launchable, and leverages what you already know.

Hustles That Start With $0

Here are proven examples of businesses you can start today with no money:

Service-Based Hustles

Social media management

Logo or graphic design

Lawn care / handyman work

Tutoring

Virtual assistance

Photography (even with a smartphone)

Knowledge-Based Hustles

Online coaching or consulting

Digital course creation (using free platforms like Teachable or Gumroad)

Writing eBooks (Amazon KDP)

Resume and cover letter services

Sales-Based Hustles

Flipping items on Facebook Marketplace, Craigslist, Mercari, or eBay

Affiliate marketing (promoting products online and earning commission)

Drop servicing (selling services you outsource)

Use What You've Got

One of the fastest ways to make money is to sell what you already own but don't use.

Go through your house and look for:

Electronics you never use

Clothes and shoes you no longer wear

Tools, sports equipment, books, or collectibles

Furniture or décor that's just taking up space

Take clear pictures, write a quick description, and post it on Facebook Marketplace, OfferUp, Craigslist, or eBay.

You'd be surprised how much cash is sitting around your house. This isn't theory—it's strategy.

Pro Tip: eBay is one of the most powerful resale platforms in the world. In 2023, eBay processed over $73 billion in sales worldwide. You don't need a storefront—you just need a PayPal or bank account and something to sell.

Personal Example: Tool Flipping

There was a time I used to go to pawn shops and flea markets and buy individual hand tools—especially those with lifetime warranties. Once I had a complete set, I'd take it to a big-box store, trade it in for brand new replacements, then sell the new set for far more than what I originally paid. It wasn't luck. It was leverage. I understood the value of the warranty and the demand for complete sets. That's a hustle.

Auction Arbitrage and Garage Sales

I also used to hit local auctions and estate sales. I'd look for undervalued items—tools, fishing gear, small appliances, and collectibles—and flip them online or at a yard sale. Anything that didn't sell online became yard sale inventory. Every dollar counted. The goal was simple: turn a little money into more money.

Real World Case: eBay's Top Sellers

The #2 eBay seller in the world (and #1 in Europe) started out buying used video games. That's it. Just flipping games online. His business exploded when he figured out how to buy in bulk and list efficiently. He didn't start with capital—he started with knowledge and volume.

The Power of AI and Online Tools

Today, you have something many of these early hustlers didn't: AI tools like ChatGPT.

You can:

Write product listings

Draft ad copy

Build a business plan

Generate niche ideas

Research competitors

All of that used to take hours—or money to outsource. Now? You've got it in your pocket.

Other tools:

Canva – Design flyers, business cards, social posts for free

Google Workspace – Run your business with Docs, Sheets, Gmail

Stripe & Square – Accept payments like a pro with no upfront cost

Linktree – Create a simple mobile landing page for your hustle

Facebook Groups & Reddit Threads – Find your audience and sell to them directly

Identify Your Skills, Then Apply Them

Take inventory of what you already know how to do:

What do people already ask you for help with?

What comes naturally to you that others find difficult?

What have you done for work, hobbies, or even favors?

Then ask: How can I turn this into a result someone would pay for?

Example: If you helped a friend write their resume and they landed a job, you've already proven value. Turn that into a hustle.

Solve Problems, Don't Just Sell Products

Money flows to solutions. Ask:

What's a pain point people around me have?

Can I solve that problem without needing to buy inventory?

Case Study: Chris Guillebeau's $100 Startup profiled dozens of people who started micro-businesses solving tiny problems—like fixing spreadsheets or writing website copy—and turned them into six-figure ventures. One woman made $32,000 in her first year selling hand-made travel gear using materials she already had.

Focus on Speed to Cash

You're not building your dream company—yet. Right now, your job is to generate cash flow. A good hustle has these characteristics:

Low or no startup cost

Quick to market

Direct access to customers

No reliance on inventory or investors

Test Fast, Fail Fast, Move Fast

Here's the framework:

1. Pick a skill, product, or niche.

2. Post your offer on free platforms (Facebook, Craigslist, Instagram, eBay, Fiverr).

3. Offer it to your personal network (friends and family, social media contacts, etc.)

4. Close your first sale—even if it's $10.

5. Repeat. Refine. Raise prices.

The sooner you get money in hand, the sooner you start thinking like a business boss instead of a dreamer.

Action Plan:

List 10 things you know how to do well.

List 10 things you could sell today (even from your garage).

Google each skill with "freelance" or "side hustle" to see real examples.

Choose 1 offer you can make publicly this week.

Post it. Tell people. Start small. Then grow fast.

Your hustle is waiting. Let's go find it—and flip it into your future.

I'm a firm believer in funding it as you go. If you have a property to rent that needs some work, rent it as is, and use the rent money to pay for the improvements. Nobody gets made when the landlord wants to make improvements! Then as the place is fixed up to the way that you want it to be you can start increasing the rent. Maybe the existing tenants will stay, maybe you will get new ones. Either way they are the ones paying to increase your revenue, not you!

As you start making sales, use the money to start paying for things like a better website, promotional tools and more advertising to increase sales even more.

Just remember that it all starts with making the first sale! You must start the wheel of revenue turning! **You do that!**

Chapter 3: Finding Your Hustle

You don't need to reinvent the wheel. You just need to find the right set of wheels to ride.

This chapter is about helping you identify a profitable hustle—something you can start with little or no money, that aligns with your skills, interests, or experience.

The Truth About Hustles

A hustle isn't just a job. It's a gateway. It's a bridge between where you are and where you're trying to go. Unlike a traditional business that may take years to build, a hustle is something you can launch in days—not months.

In a world where over 60 million Americans now work freelance (Statista, 2023), the idea of the side hustle isn't optional anymore—it's *normal*. And in many cases, it's the testing ground for a full-scale business.

But not all hustles are created equal. Some take forever to gain traction. Others burn you out before they pay off. Your job is to pick a hustle that's lean, launchable, and leverages what you already know.

Hustles That Start With $0

Here are proven examples of businesses you can start today with no money:

- **Service-Based Hustles**

  - Social media management
  - Logo or graphic design
  - Lawn care / handyman work
  - Tutoring
  - Virtual assistance
  - Photography (even with a smartphone)

- **Knowledge-Based Hustles**

  - Online coaching or consulting
  - Digital course creation (using free platforms like Teachable or Gumroad)
  - Writing eBooks (Amazon KDP)
  - Resume and cover letter services

- **Sales-Based Hustles**

  o Flipping items on Facebook Marketplace, Craigslist, Mercari, or eBay

  o Affiliate marketing (promoting products online and earning commission)

  o Drop servicing (selling services you outsource)

Use What You've Got

One of the fastest ways to make money is to sell what you already own but don't use.

Go through your house and look for:

- Electronics you never use

- Clothes and shoes you no longer wear

- Tools, sports equipment, books, or collectibles

- Furniture or décor that's just taking up space

Take clear pictures, write a quick description, and post it on Facebook Marketplace, OfferUp, Craigslist, or eBay.

You'd be surprised how much cash is sitting around your house. This isn't theory—it's strategy.

Pro Tip: eBay is one of the most powerful resale platforms in the world. In 2023, eBay processed over $73 billion in sales worldwide. You don't need a storefront—you just need a PayPal or bank account and something to sell.

Personal Example: Tool Flipping

There was a time I used to go to pawn shops and flea markets and buy individual hand tools—especially those with lifetime warranties. Once I had a complete set, I'd take it to a big-box store, trade it in for brand new replacements, then sell the new set for far more than what I originally paid. It wasn't luck. It was leverage. I understood the value of the warranty and the demand for complete sets. That's a hustle.

Auction Arbitrage and Garage Sales

I also used to hit local auctions and estate sales. I'd look for undervalued items—tools, fishing gear, small appliances, and collectibles—and flip them online or at a yard sale. Anything that didn't sell online became yard sale inventory. Every dollar counted. The goal was simple: turn a little money into more money.

Real World Case: eBay's Top Sellers

The #2 eBay seller in the world (and #1 in Europe) started out buying used video games. That's it. Just flipping games online. His business exploded when he figured out how to buy in bulk and list efficiently. He didn't start with capital—he started with *knowledge* and *volume*.

The Power of AI and Online Tools

Today, you have something many of these early hustlers didn't: **AI tools like ChatGPT.**

You can:

- Write product listings
- Draft ad copy
- Build a business plan
- Generate niche ideas
- Research competitors

All of that used to take hours—or money to outsource. Now? You've got it in your pocket.

Other tools:

- **Canva** – Design flyers, business cards, social posts for free
- **Google Workspace** – Run your business with Docs, Sheets, Gmail

- **Stripe & Square** – Accept payments like a pro with no upfront cost

- **Linktree** – Create a simple mobile landing page for your hustle

- **Facebook Groups & Reddit Threads** – Find your audience and sell to them directly

Identify Your Skills, Then Apply Them

Take inventory of what you already know how to do:

- What do people already ask you for help with?

- What comes naturally to you that others find difficult?

- What have you done for work, hobbies, or even favors?

Then ask: *How can I turn this into a result someone would pay for?*

Example: If you helped a friend write their resume and they landed a job, you've already proven value. Turn that into a hustle.

Solve Problems, Don't Just Sell Products

Money flows to solutions. Ask:

- What's a pain point people around me have?

- Can I solve that problem without needing to buy inventory?

Case Study: Chris Guillebeau's $100 Startup profiled dozens of people who started micro-businesses solving tiny problems—like fixing spreadsheets or writing website copy—and turned them into six-figure ventures. One woman made $32,000 in her first year selling hand-made travel gear using materials she already had.

Focus on Speed to Cash

You're not building your dream company—*yet.* Right now, your job is to generate *cash flow*. A good hustle has these characteristics:

- Low or no startup cost

- Quick to market

- Direct access to customers

- No reliance on inventory or investors

Test Fast, Fail Fast, Move Fast

Here's the framework:

1. Pick a skill, product, or niche.

2. Post your offer on free platforms (Facebook, Craigslist, Instagram, eBay, Fiverr).

3. Offer it to your personal network.

4. Close your first sale—even if it's $10.

5. Repeat. Refine. Raise prices.

The sooner you get money in hand, the sooner you start thinking like a business boss instead of a dreamer.

Action Plan:

- List 10 things you know how to do well.

- List 10 things you could sell today (even from your garage).

- Google each skill with "freelance" or "side hustle" to see real examples.

- Choose 1 offer you can make publicly *this week*.

- Post it. Tell people. Start small. Then grow fast.

Your hustle is waiting. Let's go find it—and flip it into your future.

Just remember, even the weighted yellow flags that the referees throw in the NFL are all made in the living room of a little old lady in Florida. Anyone can have a side hustle!

Chapter 4: From Idea to Execution

Having an idea is exciting—but turning that idea into income is what separates the dreamers from the doers.

This chapter is about how to take your hustle idea and validate it fast without spending a dime. No fancy launches, no business cards, and definitely no time wasted overthinking. Execution wins. Every time.

First, Stop Falling in Love With the Idea

You might think you have a million-dollar idea—but until someone actually pays you for it, it's just a theory.

According to a 2023 report by CB Insights, the #1 reason startups fail (cited by 42% of failed founders) is lack of market demand. In plain English: they built something nobody wanted. That's why we validate ideas early—before we spend time and money.

Don't go looking for a "great idea." Instead, look for a real problem to solve. A profitable business starts with pain. If your market isn't in pain, they're not going to pay.

Even the biggest brands in the world are built around perceived pain:

Starbucks isn't selling great coffee. In fact, multiple blind taste tests—including a Consumer Reports study—ranked it lower than McDonald's and Dunkin'. What they're selling is status and belonging. Their entire marketing machine is built on the idea that if you don't have a Starbucks cup, you're not modern, productive, or stylish.

Apple's iPhone often introduces features years after Samsung—but dominates the U.S. smartphone market. Why? Because they've convinced customers that not having an iPhone puts you behind. They've created a fear of being left out. That's a pain point. And people pay to avoid that pain.

So ask yourself: what pain does your idea solve?

You can either find a pain that's already there— or spend money to create the pain through marketing.

If you're low on budget, the answer is simple: find the pain that's already there and offer the relief.

Step 1: Define the Result

Your product or service isn't the thing. The result it delivers is what people pay for.

Don't say, "I want to start a résumé business." Say, "I help people land interviews by rewriting their résumés."

Don't say, "I'm starting a tutoring business." Say, "I help high school students boost their SAT scores by 150+ points in under 30 days."

FACT: Clear, outcome-driven offers outperform vague general services in every market. In 2022, copywriting platform Copyhackers found that conversion rates increased by over 200% when businesses focused their headlines on the end result, not just the service.

Step 2: Validate with Conversations

Don't build anything yet. Just talk to 5–10 people who would be your ideal customer. Ask them:

"What's your biggest frustration with [insert niche]?"

"Have you ever paid for help with this? If not, why?"

"If someone could solve this for you quickly, what would that be worth?"

You're not selling yet—you're listening. If they get animated, frustrated, or excited while talking, you're on to something.

Example: If you're thinking of launching a dog-walking service, ask dog owners: "What's the biggest hassle about walking your dog every day?" If they say, "I just don't have the time," then boom—your pitch becomes, "I give busy dog owners their evenings back."

Step 3: Offer the Solution BEFORE It's Perfect

Most people wait to launch until it's "ready." That's a trap. Launch it ugly. Sell before it's built. You're not lying—you're testing.

You can say: "I'm putting together a small beta group of clients for [service], and offering a steep discount in exchange for feedback. Want in?"

FACT: This method works. It's how many SaaS companies build products today. In tech, it's called a minimum viable product (MVP). Dropbox famously launched their business with a 3-minute demo video—before they built the actual software.

Step 4: Get the First Dollar

There's a world of difference between someone saying "That's cool" and someone handing you money. The moment someone pays, your idea becomes real.

That $10 transaction is more important than 1,000 likes or compliments. It means someone values what you're offering.

Your mission: Close your first sale ASAP.

Use:

Facebook Groups

Nextdoor

Instagram DMs

LinkedIn posts

Texts to people in your network

Don't forget you can always knock on doors!

Post your offer with a simple result:

> "I'm helping small businesses turn boring Instagram pages into content that brings in leads. I'm offering 5 discounted sessions. DM me if you want in."

Step 5: Use Free Platforms to Deliver the Work

You don't need a website or LLC to start. Use tools that are already available:

Google Docs/Sheets/Slides – for proposals, invoices, or deliverables

Zoom or Google Meet – for meetings

Canva – for quick design work

ChatGPT – for scripting emails, ad copy, product descriptions

Stripe, PayPal, or Square – to accept payment

These tools are trusted by millions. In fact, as of 2024, Google Workspace alone had over 3 billion users globally. You're not being "cheap" by using them—you're being smart.

Step 6: Get Feedback and Iterate

Ask your first customer what they loved and what confused them. Use that data to tweak your offer.

Repeat this 3–5 times and you'll have:

A real service or product that solves a clear problem

Proof that people will pay

Testimonials or reviews to use in future marketing

Execution > Planning

Planning feels productive. But execution is what makes money.

Case Study: In 2014, Nick Huber started a student storage business while still in college. His first step? He knocked on dorm doors and asked students if they wanted help storing their stuff for the summer. The result? A seven-figure storage company—and a blueprint he later sold as a business course.

No investors. No marketing agency. Just execution.

Action Plan:

1. Reframe your idea around a result.

2. Find the pain behind that result.

3. Talk to at least 5 real people in your market.

4. Post a public offer with limited slots.

5. Deliver it using free tools.

6. Collect testimonials.

7. Improve and repeat.

Your idea only matters if you move on it. Pain creates urgency—and urgency drives sales.

Let's get it done.

Chapter 5: The $0 Startup Toolkit

You don't need a massive budget or a full-time team to start your business. You need the right tools—and most of them are free.

This chapter breaks down the exact platforms, software, and services you can use to build, run, and grow your business from scratch without spending a dime. These tools are used by solopreneurs, startups, and even multi-million dollar brands to test ideas, manage clients, create marketing, and take payments.

Let's build your zero-cost toolbox so you can operate like a pro from day one.

1. Communication & Scheduling

Google Workspace (Docs, Sheets, Slides, Forms) – Free with a Gmail account. Over 3 billion users globally rely on this platform for professional and business use.

Zoom / Google Meet – Free virtual meetings and calls.

Calendly – Free appointment scheduling tool.

2. Payments & Invoicing

PayPal, Stripe, and Square – Industry-standard tools to accept online payments.

Wave Accounting – Free accounting and invoicing for small businesses.

3. Design & Branding

Canva – Over 135 million users. Design everything from logos to social media posts.

Adobe Express – Free version available. Great for creating high-quality graphics and scheduling social media posts.

Remove.bg – Remove image backgrounds instantly.

4. Websites & Landing Pages

Carrd.co, Wix, Weebly, WordPress.com – All offer free website builders with templates.

Google Sites – Often overlooked, but completely free and extremely easy to use with your Gmail account. No ads. No coding.

Linktree / Beacon / Solo.to – Great for social media link hubs.

ChatGPT – Here's the kicker: ChatGPT can write your website's HTML code for you. All you have to do is tell it what kind of page you want—what sections, what text, what buttons—and it will generate clean HTML code. You copy, paste, and launch. No developer required.

5. Social Media Tools

Meta Business Suite, Buffer, CapCut, InShot —
Create and schedule content across platforms.

6. Productivity & Task Management

Trello, Notion, Google Keep, and ChatGPT —
Organize, brainstorm, manage, and execute with
free apps.

7. Research & Validation

Google Trends, AnswerThePublic, Facebook
Groups, Reddit Threads — Research demand, test
offers, and learn how your audience talks.

Real Talk: This Isn't Long-Term

Let's be clear: This setup is meant to get you
started, not to support a growing company with
payroll, inventory, and legal exposure.

Yes, there are legal, tax, and marketing details that will need to be addressed down the road. That's okay. Don't get stuck in analysis paralysis trying to perfect everything on day one.

As General George S. Patton once said: "A good plan violently executed now is better than a perfect plan executed next week."

This book is about getting to action. You can pivot later. You can upgrade later. You can build out the perfect structure later. But if you don't start, someone else will.

Personal Note: I can't count how many times I've had an idea that I sat on, overthought, or waited to "perfect"—only to see someone else launch it and profit. That's a hard lesson. It's one thing I'm writing this book to help you avoid.

Action Plan:

1. Create a business Gmail account.

2. Build a simple landing page using Google Sites, Carrd, or Wix.

3. Use ChatGPT to write your first email or website copy.

4. Design a logo with Canva or Adobe Express.

5. Accept payments via PayPal or Stripe.

6. Manage tasks in Notion or Trello.

7. Post your first offer this week.

This is how you start. Not perfect. Just powerful.

Chapter 6: Legal and Legit for Less

You don't need a lawyer on retainer or a CPA on speed dial to set your business up the right way. You just need the facts—and someone to keep you from getting scammed or stalled.

"In the middle of every difficulty lies opportunity." — Albert Einstein

When it comes to legal setup, the biggest obstacle isn't money. It's misinformation. Let's get this straight now—so you don't have to undo costly mistakes later.

Why Legal Setup Matters

You'll need a formal business structure if you want to:

Open a business bank account

Get business credit

Work with real clients or vendors

Separate your personal assets

Build credibility

Corporation vs. LLC vs. Sole Proprietor

Many people choose an LLC because it sounds easy—but facts matter:

Sole Proprietor: Easy, but offers zero liability protection. All income is taxed as personal. You're fully exposed legally.

LLC: Common but misunderstood. In most states, it costs the same or more than a corporation to form, but doesn't offer the same tax advantages or credit-building benefits. You cannot retroactively elect S Corporation status later if you miss the IRS deadline, which is within 75 days of forming your entity or within 75 days of the start of the calendar year (IRS Form 2553).

Corporation (Inc): Offers the strongest legal structure for growth, the ability to build real business credit, issue shares, and elect S Corporation tax treatment (if filed on time). Contrary to online myths, in many states, forming a corporation costs the same or less than an LLC and comes with more long-term advantages.

FACT: Corporations allow business owners to pay themselves as employees and potentially save thousands in self-employment taxes. LLCs taxed as sole proprietors cannot do this.

"An ounce of prevention is worth a pound of cure." — Benjamin Franklin

If you've read my book LLC or S-Corp? Making the Right Move for Your Business, then you already know the detailed breakdown of every state's requirements, costs, and the complete step-by-step guide for filing properly.

Skip the Headache — Get It Done Right

If you're not confident navigating this yourself or just don't want the hassle, my company offers a full business setup package:

We form your corporation in your state

We file your EIN directly with the IRS

We submit your S Corp election form (IRS Form 2553) on time

We register your Sales Tax Certificate if applicable

All for $500 + your state's filing fee. No hidden upsells. No templates. This is white-glove setup.

Or you it yourself, just Don't Pay for What's Free
There are so many scammers out there charging
you to file forms that are free to file!

After you file you will get even more scammers!

Get your EIN free at irs.gov

Check your state's official Secretary of State
website—not a third-party "business directory"

Check out my book LLC or S-Corp for a full list
of exactly who to contact where in every State.

Never pay for business license info. It's public
and usually under your city or county's tax
collector

You Still Need Contracts

Even if you're small, protect yourself:

Scope of Work

Payment Terms

Refund/Cancellation Policy

Use trusted sites like RocketLawyer, LawDepot, or Docracy to get started with templates.

"Sweat equity is the most valuable equity there is." — Mark Cuban

But you still must protect it.

Final Thought: Start Smart, But Start Now

There are legal, tax, and compliance decisions that will matter—but don't let them stop you from moving.

"A good plan violently executed now is better than a perfect plan executed next week." — General George S. Patton

Too many entrepreneurs wait too long and lose the window. I've done it. I've watched others do it. If you've got momentum—use it. Get the structure in place, even if you clean it up later.

Action Plan:

1. Decide on a business name.

2. Set up a corporation in your state (or hire us to do it).

3. File your EIN on irs.gov.

4. Submit Form 2553 for S-Corp status within 75 days.

5. Apply for any required local business licenses.

6. Open your business checking account.

7. Download and customize service contracts.

Now you're not just hustling. You're building something real.

Chapter 7: Building a Brand That Sticks

A logo doesn't make a brand.

A brand is what people remember when they can't see your logo. It's the feeling they get when they hear your name, see your post, or talk to someone you've worked with. And if you want to grow a real business—not just a hustle—you need a brand that sticks.

What a Brand Really Is (and Isn't)

A brand isn't just a color palette and some graphics. A brand is:

Your reputation

Your message

Your promise

The experience people have when they deal with you

Jeff Bezos said it best: "Your brand is what people say about you when you're not in the room."

According to a 2023 Nielsen Global Trust Report, 92% of consumers trust earned media—such as recommendations from friends and family—more than any form of advertising. That's brand power. You don't buy it. You build it.

Learn From the Greats: Nike, McDonald's, and More

Nike's swoosh isn't just a logo—it's a symbol of aspiration. It was created for just $35 in 1971, but today it represents a $30+ billion brand. Nike's strength is consistency. From athletes to lifestyle marketing, the message is always clear: victory, performance, motion.

McDonald's didn't build an empire on fine dining. They built it on consistency and brand recognition. The golden arches are now more recognizable worldwide than the Christian cross (per a global survey by Sponsorship Research International). Their colors—red and yellow—are intentionally chosen to trigger hunger and attract attention.

FACT: Consistent branding across all channels increases revenue by up to 23%, according to Lucidpress's State of Brand Consistency report (2022).

The Foundation of a Sticky Brand

If your brand is going to stick, it has to do 3 things:

1. Stand for something

2. Be consistent

3. Connect emotionally

Ask Others Before You Finalize

As a founder, you see your business through your own lens—your experiences, your goals, your vision. But the customer sees it through need and urgency. The most successful brands are built around how people think when they're looking for help.

Before you lock in a business name, logo, or tagline:

Ask at least 5–10 people what they think your business does based on the name or logo alone.

Ask what they would Google if they needed your service.

Ask what emotion the design gives them—trust, excitement, professionalism, etc.

Often, small tweaks based on this feedback can make or break your launch.

Choose a Name That's Findable and Clear

Easy to say, spell, and remember

No inside jokes, complex words, or slang

Includes keywords if possible

Check domain availability and run a trademark check at USPTO.gov

Use ChatGPT to brainstorm name ideas and taglines, and ask friends to vote on their top 3.

Create a Logo: DIY or Outsource

If you have a good eye, use:

Canva

Adobe Express

Looka

If not, go to Fiverr or Upwork and hire someone for $25–$75 to do it professionally. You only need one great version—don't get stuck in 30 revisions.

Lock In a Free Web Presence

Google Sites

Carrd.co

Wix

Linktree or Beacon for social bios

Use ChatGPT to write clean homepage text and HTML code if needed. You can build a clean, converting page in under an hour.

Tell Your Brand Story

People remember stories. Share yours:

Where you started

Who you help

What makes your method unique

"People don't buy what you do; they buy why you do it." — Simon Sinek

Use your story on your website, social bios, and even printed flyers.

Expand with Personal Branding

The most powerful marketing tool is YOU. Use your face, voice, and values to build connection.

Post:

Daily behind-the-scenes or wins

Educational content

Stories from your clients

Photos of you doing the work

Action Plan:

1. Ask 5 people how they would describe your business

2. Choose a name and tagline that matches how THEY think

3. Use Canva, Adobe Express, or Fiverr for your logo

4. Create a Linktree or free site using ChatGPT and Google Sites

5. Write and post your brand story

6. Lock in consistent bios and handles across all platforms

Branding isn't what you say about your business—it's what people repeat about your business when you're not there.

Make it sticky. Make it simple. Make it resonate.

Let's go.

Chapter 8: Getting Clients Without Ads
Proven Guerrilla Marketing Tactics

If you're trying to grow a real business, there's one thing you need to stop doing immediately: stop selling on price.

Here's the truth: customers don't buy based on the lowest price. They buy based on perceived value, trust, and connection. When you compete on price, you automatically position yourself as a commodity. And guess what happens to commodities? They're always one click away from being replaced by something cheaper.

Price-based selling attracts the wrong type of customer—those who want the most for the least. These are the people who:

Complain the most.

Demand constant discounts.

Leave the second someone cheaper pops up.

Instead of building a loyal tribe of repeat buyers, you end up babysitting bargain hunters.

"When you sell on price, you teach customers to value your product less, not more."

"Selling on price is just wrong. It cheapens you. People don't buy on price—they buy on relationship." — Eric Gilbert

Stats Don't Lie

Only 15% of buyers say price is their number one factor.

78% of customers buy based on the relationship with the brand or seller.

Loyalty programs increase repeat business by over 70%.

Businesses that use loyalty programs grow 2.5x faster than those that don't.

So What Should You Do Instead?

1. Sell the Relationship, Not the Deal

People do business with those they know, like, and trust. That means:

Show up.

Follow up.

Share your story.

Make people feel like they're buying into something bigger than a transaction.

2. Create a Loyalty Program

Reward your best clients. Give them:

First access

Exclusive deals

Invite-only events

This builds community and FOMO.

3. Offer a Value-Based Newsletter

Don't give discounts—give value. Send out a monthly newsletter to your VIPs only. Include:

Behind-the-scenes content

Pro tips

Quick wins

Success stories

Early access to new launches

Let ChatGPT help write it.

4. Host an Annual Customer Party

Throw a customer appreciation event once a year. Bring your best customers together. Let them post it, tag it, and brag about being on your invite list.

5. Leverage Referrals

Offer something for referring a friend—store credit, a free upgrade, VIP status. You don't need a discount to create loyalty.

You just need to make your best customers feel important. If they feel like you took care of them, and you make them feel important, they will want to give you referrals!

6. Position Yourself as the Expert

You can charge more when people see you as the authority. Here's how:

Write a book (it's free to self-publish on Amazon now)

Speak at local events or conferences

Host free webinars or Q&A sessions

Share case studies and client wins

You're reading this book, right? How do you think that happened?
Because I positioned myself.

What Guerrilla Marketers Know That You Don't

This is where most people miss the mark.
Guerrilla marketing isn't just about social media.
It's about:

Networking

Getting face-to-face

Owning your space

You should be at:

Local business events

Chamber meetings

Networking mixers

Street fairs and expos

Introduce yourself. Bring cards. Ask questions. Listen. Talk about what you do in a way that relates to them.

"Networking is just marketing with a handshake."

Real Authority Doesn't Compete on Price

When people see you as a leader, price becomes irrelevant. You're not the cheapest. You're the most trusted. The most valuable. The one they want.

107

Start doing webinars. Go live once a week. Write a guide. Answer questions in Facebook groups. Drop a blog post on LinkedIn. Let people see you teaching. They'll trust you faster.

If you really want to be taken seriously—write a book. It's free now. You just have to write it. Even a 30-page guide puts you in a different category.

Final Thought: Raise Your Standards

You can always be the cheapest... but then you'll always be broke.

Or—you can be the **best**. Known. Trusted. **In demand.**

Stop selling on price. Start selling like a boss.

Chapter 9: Using Social Media to Look Bigger Than You Are

How to Appear Professional and Scale Trust

"All things being equal, people will do business with, and refer business to, those people they know, like and trust."

— Bob Burg, author of Endless Referrals

Small businesses don't lose to bigger competitors because they have worse products or weaker service. They lose because the competition looks more trustworthy. In today's market, people often judge your business by your online presence before they ever walk through the door or pick up the phone. That's why knowing how to look bigger than you are can directly grow your sales and open new doors—without ever lying.

The Power of Perception

You don't need a huge team, fancy office, or $10,000 marketing budget. You need consistency, confidence, and clarity in your messaging.

According to a BrightLocal survey, 87% of consumers read online reviews before choosing a local business. 71% say they are more likely to buy from a brand they recognize. But here's the twist: that "recognition" often comes just from repetition and presentation, not actual size.

So how do you appear bigger? It's not about pretending to be someone you're not. It's about showing up like a real business—one that takes itself seriously and makes customers feel confident in buying from you.

---

1. Branding Like a Business, Not a Hobby

People support businesses they trust. And that starts with a look that feels professional and unified. This means:

A real business name (not just your personal name)

A logo that appears everywhere consistently

A matching domain email (not @gmail.com)

A modern website with easy-to-find services or products

A clean, up-to-date Google Business listing

Story:

I worked with a guy named Tim who was running a solo based business. It was good, but he was stuck. People liked him, but he couldn't grow beyond himself. We rebranded everything around Team + [His Last Name]. Suddenly, it felt like a company. He didn't need to pretend to be a big firm—he just shifted the perception. That small tweak unlocked bigger clients and allowed him to bring in contractors under the "team" umbrella without confusing the brand. Now even when his customers were dealing with one of his contractors, they still *felt* like they were dealing with Tim!

---

2. Simple Social Media = Serious Results

Most people overthink social media. They think they need to post viral videos, hold contests, or be influencers. Not true.

Statistic: Businesses that post even once a week see 33% more customer engagement than those that don't post at all.

Story:

I once coached a woman who ran a hair and beauty business. She thought marketing meant flashy promos, events, or editing apps. I told her: "Just post a photo of the hair you did today. That's it." She finally did—and someone booked her within 20 minutes. Now she stays as busy as she wants, just by sharing her real work.

That's the key: show what you do. That's enough. No sales gimmicks. No overproduction. Just consistency.

---

3. Act Bigger by Partnering and Showing Up

Collaborate with other business owners. Share each other's posts. Tag them. Attend or host networking events—even virtually. Why? Because being seen around other business owners makes people think you're part of something bigger than just you.

And don't just show up. Teach something.

Start hosting free webinars, lives, or workshops on what you know. When you educate others, they view you as an expert.

"The best marketing doesn't feel like marketing."

— Tom Fishburne, Marketoonist

One great strategy is to write a short book or guide. You can self-publish on Amazon for free, and now you're not just a business owner— you're a published expert in your field. That's the perception shift you want.

---

4. Build Trust Through Communication

Want to look bigger? Start emailing your best customers monthly with updates, tips, or exclusive offers. Not sales—value.

Don't offer discounts. That cheapens your brand.
Instead:

Run a referral rewards program

Host a customer appreciation event once a year

Give loyal clients access to a VIP newsletter or
early access

**"Discounts attract bargain hunters.
Relationships attract repeat buyers." —
Unknown**

---

5. Automate the Small Stuff

Use tools that make your one-person business feel like a team:

Calendly or Acuity for automated bookings

Canva for easy, professional graphics

Meta Business Suite or Buffer to schedule posts

ChatGPT to help write captions, emails, and product descriptions

---

Final Word

Looking bigger than you are isn't about lying.
It's about stepping into your business like it
matters—because it does.

Make it look sharp. Show up consistently. Talk
like a brand, not a hobbyist. Build relationships,
not sales funnels. You'll start attracting better
clients, and soon you'll realize you've actually
grown into the image you've been putting out all
along.

Chapter 10: Growing Fast Without Funding

Using Cash Flow, Creativity, and Leverage to Scale Smart

"You don't need money to start a business. You need a problem to solve, people to serve, and a plan to execute."

— Melinda Emerson, The SmallBizLady

Funding is not the key to growth. Strategy is. In fact, according to the U.S. Bank, 82% of small business failures are due to poor cash flow management—not lack of investment. This chapter is your roadmap to growing fast without debt, loans, or giving up equity.

---

1. Build to Profit Early—Not for Vanity Metrics

If you want to grow without funding, forget about hype. Focus on revenue. That means:

Charge from Day One—even if it's just a small fee. Free is not sustainable.

Sell what you already know or have, not what you have to build.

Validate with sales, not surveys.

"The most reliable funding source is a paying customer."

— Jason Fried, Basecamp Co-Founder

Don't waste time chasing perfection. Sell the minimum viable version of your offer. Let revenue tell you what to improve.

---

2. Leverage What You Already Have

You probably already have assets you're not using fully:

Email list: Even a few dozen people can generate sales if you communicate right.

Skills: Package your services into a product or course.

Content: Turn blogs or tips into downloadable PDFs or ebooks.

Social media: Organic reach is still free. Use it.

Stat: A McKinsey report found that word-of-mouth and referrals drive 20% to 50% of all purchasing decisions, making your network a growth engine with zero ad spend.

---

3. Use Cash Flow to Fund Growth

You don't need a loan when you have customers. The key is using each sale to fund the next move.

Example:

You land a $1,000 client.

You set aside $200 for ads, $100 for tools, and $100 for design upgrades.

That $400 reinvestment fuels the next $2,000 month.

This snowballs. The faster your turnaround, the faster you grow. That's called a cash conversion cycle—the time it takes for money spent to come back as profit. Keep it tight.

**"Profit is not something to add on at the end—
it's something to plan for in advance."**

— Mike Michalowicz, Profit First

---

4. Partner Smart

If you can't afford to hire, partner with people
who have skills you lack. This can be temporary,
project-based, or even barter.

Photographer needs a website? Offer to build it
in exchange for product photos.

Marketer needs help with logistics? Trade for
copywriting or strategy.

Consultant wants to launch a course? Split
revenue in exchange for building the backend.

Stat: 54% of businesses in the U.S. use some form of strategic partnership or outsourcing to scale without taking on full-time staff (Source: SCORE, 2022).

---

5. Focus on Recurring Revenue Models

Growth is hard when you start from zero every month. But subscription or retainer-based models give you predictable cash flow to reinvest.

Some ideas:

Coaching or services on monthly retainers

VIP memberships or access-only communities

Subscription boxes or digital product clubs

Maintenance or update plans

> "Make money while you sleep" isn't magic—
it's math. Recurring revenue adds stability.

Even if your business is service-based, find a
way to offer something ongoing.

---

6. Sell Before You Build

This is one of the fastest ways to grow without
debt: pre-sell.

Whether it's a course, a physical product, or a
coaching program—sell it first, build it after.

Use landing pages to test interest.

126

Run small test launches with beta access.

Offer early bird discounts (but never discounts just to sell).

Stat: According to HubSpot, 68% of businesses that pre-launch with a waitlist or beta test convert at a higher rate than those who don't.

This is real proof of demand—and it brings in revenue before expenses.

---

7. Invest Time Instead of Money

When money is tight, hustle has to be high. The good news is, some of the most effective growth channels are free:

Cold outreach on LinkedIn, email, or DM

Free value posts on Facebook groups or niche forums

Strategic commenting on content your audience already follows

Public speaking at local events or online workshops

You don't have to scale by spending. You can scale by showing up—smart and loud.

---

8. Avoid the Trap of Funding Addiction

Be careful what you wish for. Getting capital too early can destroy your business. Why?

You scale before you're ready.

You lose focus trying to please investors.

You build bloat instead of profit.

> "Startups that bootstrap are more likely to be financially disciplined, customer-focused, and sustainable."

— CB Insights

Growing fast without funding forces you to be lean, scrappy, and efficient—and those are traits of businesses that last.

Real Talk: Funding Comes With Pressure

Remember, being broke can have its advantages.

When you don't have a pile of money, you're forced to make smart, fast decisions and to

129

listen to your customers instead of chasing trends.

Here's a real-world perspective:

Many successful entrepreneurs have started multiple businesses, acquired companies, and sold others for a solid profit—without ever taking a loan or getting outside investment. That's not luck. That's leverage.

Now, there are certainly larger projects and companies that require big funding. Some ventures do need $1M+ capital injections, and pitching investors becomes part of the job. But that's a completely different playing field than most solo entrepreneurs or first-time small business owners are in.

In a startup's early stages, the biggest threat to success is pressure. When you're already overwhelmed figuring out how to get clients, hire help, manage cash flow, and build systems, the last thing you need is a loan payment breathing down your neck.

If there's any way to start your business without a loan—do it.

Even if it means moving slower for a few months. You'll own more, owe less, and sleep better.

Final Word

You don't need a bank loan, a silent partner, or a shark to succeed.

You need to think creatively, use what you have, move fast, and build with the goal of making every dollar work like ten. This isn't about luck— it's about leverage.

Grow on your terms. Grow profit-first. Grow now.

Chapter 11: When to Hire, Fire, and Partner

Making Smart People Decisions Without
Breaking Your Business

**"The secret to scaling a business isn't doing
more—it's doing less of the wrong things with
the wrong people."**

— Verne Harnish, Scaling Up

People decisions make or break businesses.
Hiring too soon, firing too late, or choosing the
wrong partner can sink even the most promising
business idea.

This chapter breaks down how to know when it's
time to hire help, when it's necessary to fire
quickly, and how to partner strategically—even
with limited resources.

1. When to Hire

Hiring too early = unnecessary payroll drain.

Hiring too late = burnout and missed opportunities.

According to the U.S. Chamber of Commerce, 38% of small business owners say labor costs are their biggest monthly expense. Hiring has to be driven by clear math—not feelings.

Hire when:

You're consistently turning down paid work because you're at capacity

You're spending more than 30% of your time on low-value tasks

You can clearly define the role, goals, and ROI within 60–90 days

You can afford at least 3–6 months of payroll without new revenue

"Don't hire to grow. Hire to stop the bleeding of time."

— Paul Jarvis, author of Company of One

Start with contractors. You don't need a full-time team. Freelancers, VAs, and part-time help can bridge the gap without committing to benefits, payroll taxes, or office space.

---

2. Do a Real-Time Study of Your Workload

Before you hire anyone, you need to take an honest look at where your time is actually going.

Look at how you spend your time each day. Do a real time study for one week. Write down what you do throughout each day (all day—not just your written hours, because I know you're taking work home). Write it down in 5- or 15-minute intervals. At the end of the week, add everything up to see where your time is actually going. This will give you a real clue how you're spending your time.

Once you have that, put your time into buckets—sales, marketing, fulfillment, admin, customer service—and see if there are buckets that you can hand off to someone else.

You can start by hiring services for some of those things. That may be more expensive than having an employee do it in-house, but when you decide to hire someone, you can move those buckets in-house based on the skillset of who you hire.

> The advantage of hiring services (like a marketing firm) is that you're getting experts in that field, and all you have to do is review the reports. Now your time bucket is freed up to sell and generate more cash—or whatever your high payoff activity is.

Eventually, the goal should be to keep replacing yourself so that you can live just doing what you enjoy!

Again, if you need help in this area, I have helped clients restructure their companies by restructuring their use of time—and in so doing, they get to watch their companies grow each year while they get to spend more time doing what they love! Feel free to reach out to me if you need help with your time study, it could help make millions!

3. Who to Hire First

If you're solo, your first hire should replace your lowest-value time.

Stat: A 2022 QuickBooks survey found that small business owners spend an average of 16 hours per week on admin and operations tasks.

That's two full days per week you're not selling or creating value.

Start by outsourcing:

Admin tasks (invoicing, email, scheduling)

Social media posting (not strategy—just posting)

Bookkeeping

Customer service responses

If you're a service-based business, hiring another producer (designer, tech, stylist, etc.) who can replicate your offer is often the best way to double revenue without doubling effort.

4. When to Fire

The cost of a bad hire isn't just the salary. It's lost time, lost momentum, and potential brand damage.

Stat: The U.S. Department of Labor estimates the cost of a bad hire is at least 30% of the employee's first-year earnings. Other sources peg it at over $15,000 for small businesses.

Fire when:

They miss deadlines or ignore expectations— even after clear conversations

Clients or team members report repeated issues

Their presence adds stress, confusion, or negativity to your business

You're spending more time fixing their work than doing your own

"Hire slow. Fire fast. Regret nothing." — Anonymous

How to fire responsibly:

Document all performance issues and warnings

Stay professional, not emotional

Don't delay—protect the culture and your sanity

Letting go of the wrong person frees you to attract the right one.

---

5. When to Partner

Don't partner because you're lonely. Partner because it's leverage.

A true partnership brings a skill set, resource, audience, or capital that accelerates growth. It should not duplicate what you already do. Partners should complement, not clone.

"The best partnerships are built on mutual goals and opposite strengths."

— Harvard Business Review

Partner when:

You have aligned values but different superpowers

You're entering a new market or launching a new product you can't build alone

The other person brings access—clients, investors, or tech

There's a clear agreement in writing (ALWAYS in writing)

Red flags:

You feel pressured into it

One party is more committed than the other

You haven't worked on a project together yet

No written terms on money, decisions, or exit plan

Even strategic partnerships—like cross-promotions or rev-share deals—should be treated with legal structure and professional expectations.

---

6. Employees vs. Contractors

Stat: According to the IRS, misclassifying employees as contractors is one of the top tax violations for small businesses, leading to thousands in back taxes and penalties.

Use contractors when:

The work is project-based or temporary

You don't need to control their schedule or tools

You're not providing benefits, uniforms, or ongoing supervision

Use employees when:

You dictate when, where, and how the work is done

They are part of daily operations and decisions

You need them available consistently for long-term tasks

When in doubt, consult a tax professional. Getting this wrong can crush a growing business.

---

7. Leadership vs. Delegation

Hiring or partnering doesn't mean you stop doing the hard stuff. It means you do more of the right things.

"If you want to go fast, go alone. If you want to go far, go together."

— African Proverb

But the goal isn't just delegation—it's leadership. Your job is to cast the vision, define outcomes, and protect the culture. Growth requires people, but sustainable growth requires the right people in the right roles.

Final Word

Growing a business is not just about doing more. It's about doing less of the wrong things and bringing in the right help at the right time.

Hire slow. Fire fast. Partner wisely.

And never forget: your time is your most valuable resource. Guard it, measure it, and invest it where it creates the biggest return.

Chapter 12: Making the Leap Full-Time

How to Leave Your Job Without Losing Your Mind (or Your Mortgage)

"Don't burn your bridges until you've built a boat."

— Unknown

One of the biggest questions entrepreneurs face is: "When should I go full-time?"

It's a critical moment that separates a side hustle from a real business. But jumping too soon—or waiting too long—can hurt your finances, your confidence, and your company.

This chapter breaks down exactly how to know when you're ready, how to plan the exit, and how to survive the emotional rollercoaster that comes with betting on yourself.

---

1. The Myth of "All In"

You don't have to quit your job today to be serious about your business.

According to a 2021 LinkedIn study, 33% of full-time entrepreneurs started their businesses as side hustles for at least 6–12 months before going full-time. In fact, many successful founders held onto their 9–5 until they could no longer scale part-time.

Going full-time should be a financial decision, not an emotional one.

"Never jump off a cliff and hope you learn to fly on the way down."

— Barbara Corcoran, Shark Tank

---

2. Know Your Numbers First

Before you quit, you need to be brutally honest with your money.

Ask yourself:

How much money do I need per month just to survive?

What's the bare minimum my business can generate consistently?

How many months of expenses do I have saved up?

What happens if I earn nothing for 60 days?

Stat: A survey by Bankrate shows that only 44% of Americans could cover a $1,000 emergency with savings. If you're not part of that 44%, you're not ready yet.

Your goal: Build at least 3–6 months of business + personal runway before you quit your job. That's your "freedom fund."

---

3. Prove the Concept First

Don't assume your idea will work full-time just because it feels good part-time.

Before you leap, prove that:

You've had at least 3 paying clients or sales

You can attract customers without personal referrals

You've worked with a stranger who paid full price

You've handled the delivery, marketing, and support yourself

"A business isn't real until strangers are buying."

— Chris Guillebeau, The $100 Startup

If you're not consistently landing business while part-time, going full-time won't solve the problem—it'll magnify it.

---

4. Transition with a Plan, Not a Panic

Quitting your job doesn't have to be dramatic. The smartest exits are planned.

Here's how to structure a real transition:

1. Set a target date, 3–6 months out.

2. Start building systems: automate tasks, test pricing, get feedback.

3. Cut personal expenses: simplify your lifestyle so less income is required.

4. Build recurring revenue: subscriptions, retainers, or predictable clients.

5. Talk to your boss (if possible): Some jobs will let you reduce hours or freelance part-time.

"Plan your exit like a product launch. Not a breakup."

— Marie Forleo

5. Shift Your Mindset: You're the Employer Now

The hardest part of going full-time isn't
financial—it's mental.

You are no longer getting paid to show up.
You're getting paid for results.

That means:

You pay for your own tools, taxes, and time

You eat what you kill (no sales = no paycheck)

You must replace structure with discipline

You stop asking for permission

Stat: According to FreshBooks, 62% of new
entrepreneurs say the hardest part of self-
employment is managing time and staying
motivated.

Create a schedule. Set real working hours. Track goals weekly. Treat yourself like your own employee until your business has enough structure to run without constant hustle.

6. Discipline is the Difference

You have to treat your business as seriously as you would a job.

That means showing up on time, staying productive, and holding yourself accountable—like you could be fired for poor performance.

During the early days, be extremely careful with your personal money. Don't spend what you don't need to. Eat at home—it's cheaper and healthier. Pack a lunch. Bring drinks from home when you go out. Every dollar saved is a dollar that can help fund your new business.

Also, don't confuse sitting at the computer with working. Most people don't make money pushing buttons—they make money talking to people.

Getting in front of people or getting on the phone is what creates sales.

Don't make excuses or wait for someone to "discover" you.

Get in gear and start working like your life depends on it—because the life of your business does.

"Discipline equals freedom."

— Jocko Willink

7. It's Not Forever—It's a Phase

Going full-time is a big step, but it's not the final step.

It's just one phase in the larger journey from survival to growth to freedom.

Some people romanticize quitting. But others go full-time too soon and quietly go broke. Remember, the goal isn't to just work for yourself—the goal is to build something that eventually works without you.

"Entrepreneurs are willing to work 80 hours a week to avoid working 40 for someone else."

— Lori Greiner

That may be true at first. But you shouldn't glorify burnout. Plan to grow into working smarter, not harder, as soon as systems allow.

Final Word

Going full-time in your business can be the most liberating—and terrifying—decision you ever make. But if you:

Know your numbers,

Prove your product or service,

Build savings,

Cut waste,

And plan your exit wisely...

Then it can also be the smartest move of your career.

Don't leap blind. Walk out with a plan. Then run like hell with focus.

Chapter 13: From Side Hustle to Real Hustle

Turning Your Nights and Weekends into a Scalable Business

"Every big business started as someone's side hustle."

— Forbes

The difference between a hobby and a business isn't passion—it's structure, profitability, and accountability. In this chapter, we're going to break down exactly how to shift from dabbling on the side to operating like a legitimate business, even if you're still working a day job.

This isn't just about working harder. It's about putting real systems in place, building consistency, and treating your hustle like it already deserves to win.

1. A Side Hustle Isn't Just a Start—It's a Test

Stat: According to a 2022 Zapier survey, 1 in 3 Americans has a side hustle, and 67% of them started it to earn extra income, not to quit their job. But only a small percentage ever make the shift to full-time.

Why? Because they treat it like a side project, not a business-in-training.

"Side hustles are the modern-day apprenticeship."

— Fast Company

If your goal is to grow, your side hustle must be set up like a business from the beginning:

Have a business name, bank account, and EIN

Track revenue and expenses professionally

Block off specific time on your calendar—this isn't a "when I have time" thing

---

2. Get Serious About Systems

Most side hustles fail to scale because they run on guesswork. If you're going to transition into real income, you need to treat your time, money, and processes seriously.

Set up:

A lead generation system (email, DM outreach, paid ads, content marketing)

A sales funnel or conversion path (website, booking page, checkout)

A client delivery system (templates, SOPs, automated follow-ups)

From your previous materials:

"If you're too busy doing the work to build the business, you'll always be stuck doing the work."

— LLC or S-Corp? Making the Right Move for Your Business
Eric F Gilbert

You cannot scale chaos. If it lives in your head, it's not scalable. Put it in writing.

3. Package, Don't Just Hustle

Trading time for money will cap your income.
Most side hustlers charge by the hour and
wonder why they never break through.

To level up:

Turn services into packages. (e.g., Instead of
"$50/hour for social media help," try
"$400/month for 3 posts/week + engagement")

Create digital products (guides, templates, mini-
courses)

Offer retainer options for ongoing work

Stat: According to PayPal, creators and
solopreneurs who switch to packaged pricing
see a 27% increase in earnings within the first 3
months.

People don't buy hours. They buy outcomes.

4. Make Money Before You Scale

Don't fall into the trap of building big before you're profitable. No one cares how professional your logo looks if your product doesn't solve a problem.

Use your side hustle to validate before investing in:

Custom websites

Fancy marketing funnels

Office space or staff

"Don't scale until it hurts not to."

— Eric Ries, The Lean Startup

Instead, focus on:

Selling one offer repeatedly

Getting repeat customers

Refining your delivery until it's easy to hand off

---

5. Protect Your Time Ruthlessly

The biggest challenge for side hustlers? Time.

"You can always make more money. You can't make more time."

— Jim Rohn

If you want your side hustle to become your main hustle, you'll have to say no to a lot of things:

Late nights scrolling

Netflix binges

Social obligations that drain energy

This isn't forever—but this is what it takes.

Tip from your earlier chapters: Do a real-time audit of how you spend your time each week. Break it into buckets. Start cutting out the low-payoff activities and focus on lead generation, conversions, and delivery.

6. Register Your Business Before It Grows

From LLC or S-Corp? Making the Right Move for Your Business, you break it down clearly:

"If you're making over $500/month, you should seriously consider forming a legal business entity. It's not about looking official—it's about protecting your assets and opening doors to scale."
Eric F Gilbert

Side hustlers often wait too long to get legit. But with low-cost options like LLCs or S-Corps—and platforms like Sunbiz.org or Stripe Atlas—there's no excuse to delay.

Stat: According to the SBA, businesses that incorporate early are 78% more likely to receive business credit or qualify for small business grants.

7. Stop Hiding—Start Marketing

A lot of side hustlers never break through because they're quietly working in the background. If no one knows what you do, you'll stay small.

Start posting consistently about your work

Tell your story in your content

Build a basic website with booking/contact forms

Ask for reviews from your earliest happy customers

You don't need to be a marketing genius. You need to be visible.

"The best product in the world will sit on the shelf if no one knows it's there."

— Donald Miller, StoryBrand

8. Treat It Like It's Already Real

"Work until your side hustle pays all your bills. Then work some more so you never have to look back."

— Anonymous

Here's the truth: you won't "find time" for your side hustle. You'll have to fight for it.

You have to:

Show up consistently

Stick to deadlines

Meet goals even when no one's watching

Treat yourself like a boss or fire yourself like one.

Don't expect a full-time business to come out of part-time effort forever. But if you build it right, your hustle won't just replace your job—it'll change your life.

Final Word

A side hustle is the perfect test bed for what your business could become.

When you commit to structure, validate your offer, package your service, and protect your time, you lay the foundation for a business that grows with or without you.

Don't treat your side hustle like a side note. Treat it like your main thing—just waiting to break through.

Chapter 14: The Business Boss Blueprint

The Exact Systems, Mindsets, and Moves You Need to Run a Profitable Business That Doesn't Run You

"You don't rise to the level of your goals. You fall to the level of your systems."

— James Clear, Atomic Habits

At this point in the book, you've learned how to start lean, grow fast, delegate smart, and make the leap full-time. But now it's time to think like a business boss, not just a solo hustler.

This chapter lays out the Business Boss Blueprint—a step-by-step structure you can follow to run your business like a well-oiled machine that scales and survives without breaking you in the process.

1. Treat Your Business Like a Business—Not a Job

"Most people never get rich from their business because they're too busy working *in it* instead of *on it.*"
Eric F Gilbert

To run a real business, you have to:

Pay yourself on a structured schedule (W-2 or Owner's Draw)

Separate your personal and business finances completely

Create a budget for both operations and marketing

Assign job descriptions—even if you're the one doing them all at first

Stat: According to QuickBooks, 65% of small business owners mix personal and business finances, which leads to cash flow confusion, tax issues, and poor decisions.

A real business has structure. Make time each month to review:

Profit & loss

Customer feedback

Conversion data

Systems breakdowns

2. Set Up Systems to Scale

"If it's not written down, it's not a system. It's a habit—and habits fail under pressure."

Eric F Gilbert

You need to systematize your business like you're preparing to hand it off—even if you're not there yet.

Key systems every business boss should have:

Lead capture (email forms, call-to-actions, landing pages)

Sales pipeline (CRM, quote templates, automated follow-up)

Fulfillment workflow (step-by-step delivery processes)

Customer onboarding and offboarding

Referral and review generation

Use simple tools at first: Google Docs, Trello, Calendly, Stripe, Notion.

Later, upgrade into platforms like ClickUp, Dubsado, or HubSpot as you grow.

Stat: Businesses with documented systems and SOPs scale 30% faster and operate with 27% fewer internal errors, according to Process.st.

3. Build in Recurring Revenue Early

One-time sales don't build wealth. Recurring revenue creates predictability, stability, and scalability.

"Build your business model around how you want to live. If you want freedom, you need cash flow that doesn't rely on constant chasing."

Eric F Gilbert

Recurring revenue models:

Retainers (for services)

Subscriptions (digital products, community access)

Maintenance plans (websites, products, support)

Licensing or royalties (intellectual property, courses)

Stat: According to a 2023 McKinsey report, companies with over 40% recurring revenue have twice the survival rate through market downturns.

4. Know Your Numbers Cold

"You can't grow what you don't measure."
Eric F Gilbert

Track these weekly:

Revenue by product or service

Conversion rate (leads to sales)

Customer acquisition cost (CAC)

Lifetime customer value (LTV)

Net profit margin

Stat: According to SCORE, businesses that review their finances monthly are 78% more likely to hit their annual revenue targets.

Set goals, not just dreams.

Instead of "I want to make $10K/month," break
it into:

How many clients do you need?

At what average price point?

What close rate do you need from your leads?

Then reverse-engineer your marketing and
outreach plan from there.

---

5. Don't DIY Everything Forever

The goal isn't to do more—it's to do less with higher value.

"Figure out your high-payoff activities and delegate the rest. That's how businesses scale and lives get better."
Eric F Gilbert

You should aim to replace yourself in the following order:

1. Admin tasks (email, invoicing, scheduling)

2. Fulfillment (service or product delivery)

3. Sales (lead qualification, onboarding)

4. Marketing (ads, social media, SEO)

Use freelancers, VAs, or agencies until it makes sense to bring roles in-house.

Your time should eventually focus on:

Strategy

Relationships

Sales conversion

Leadership

---

6. Build Authority and Influence

"People don't buy just because of price—they buy based on trust. Show them you know what you're talking about."
Eric F Gilbert

Ways to position yourself as the go-to expert:

Write a book (like this one)

Launch a podcast or YouTube series

Host free webinars and paid trainings

Speak at local or virtual events

Get featured in articles or podcasts

Stat: 84% of people say they're more likely to buy from a business owner who's published content, according to Content Marketing Institute.

People want to buy from leaders, not lurkers.

7. Build a Brand, Not Just a Business

"Brand is what people say about you when you're not in the room."

— Jeff Bezos

Your brand is more than your logo. It's:

Your tone of voice

The problems you solve

The customer experience you deliver

The story people tell about working with you

From your client work and marketing firm:

Be consistent across all platforms

Use content to show values and personality

Create a signature phrase, offer, or hook that
people remember

Brand loyalty beats price sensitivity—every time.

Final Word

A real business doesn't run on energy drinks and grit. It runs on:

Systems

Structure

Strategy

Standards

You don't need to do everything at once. But every week, move closer to a business that earns consistently, serves predictably, and scales sustainably.

That's what it means to be a Business Boss.

Chapter 15: If You Had to Start Again Tomorrow

The Rebuild Blueprint for Entrepreneurs Who Aren't Afraid to Work

"You don't need more resources. You need to be more resourceful."

— Tony Robbins

Every successful entrepreneur has asked the question at least once: "If I had to start all over, what would I do differently?"

It's a powerful exercise—because it reveals what truly works and strips away everything that doesn't.

This chapter is your tactical playbook for starting again from zero—with only your skills, your work ethic, and your brain. No investors. No favors. No fluff.

1. Start With What You Know Sells

"Don't start with what you love. Start with what you know people are already paying for."

— From LLC or S-Corp? Making the Right Move for Your Business

The fastest path to profit is to sell something people already want—especially if you've delivered it before.

If starting from scratch:

Write down every result you've helped someone get in the past (formally or informally).

Find the one you can package up and sell right now—no tech, no overhead.

Charge money for it immediately. Not in 30 days. Today.

Stat: According to Forbes, the #1 reason startups fail is "no market need"—accounting for 35% of failures.

Don't build what people might want. Sell what they already search for.

2. Get Legal, Get Real, Get Paid

"You can form an LLC, get an EIN, and open a bank account in one day. There's no excuse not to start as a real business."
- Eric F Gilbert

Register an LLC in your state (start with Sunbiz.org in Florida)

Get your free EIN from IRS.gov (do not pay a service for this)

Open a dedicated business bank account

Use Stripe or Square to start accepting payments within 24 hours

Stat: Businesses with separate business banking and legal structure are more than twice as likely to access funding and grow sustainably (Source: U.S. Small Business Administration).

Even if you're starting small, do it right from the beginning.

3. Sell Direct Before You Build Infrastructure

You don't need a website. You need clients.

Day 1 strategy:

Reach out to 50 people via text, DM, or email and tell them what you're offering.

Post three times a day on Facebook, Instagram, or LinkedIn.

Offer a simple, fast result (e.g., "I can help you get [specific result] in 48 hours.")

Take payment with a mobile invoice.

"Sales come from conversations, not configurations."

— Eric F Gilbert

Focus on getting your first sale—not building the perfect system.

4. Price Based on Value, Not Time

If you're rebuilding, you can't afford to charge hourly. You need cash and clarity.

Create 1–2 simple, outcome-based offers.

Price based on result, not time.

Create 3 price tiers (starter, standard, premium).

Stat: According to FreshBooks, freelancers and solo service providers who switch to value-based packages earn 34% more and retain more clients long-term.

> "People don't pay for hours. They pay for transformation."
> - Eric F Gilbert

If you've helped someone get results before, you're already qualified.

5. Create a Real Offer—Not Just a Skill

> "Nobody buys 'graphic design.' They buy a better brand, more clicks, or a professional edge."
>
> — Eric F Gilbert

You don't sell skills. You sell outcomes.

Use this formula to package your rebuilt offer: I help [WHO] get [RESULT] without [PAIN].

Examples:

"I help realtors get more listings using Instagram without wasting money on ads."

"I help small business owners form their LLC and EIN in 3 days with zero confusion."

"I help stylists stay booked using my 3-step content formula—no dancing required."

Make it clear. Make it specific. Make it urgent.

6. Rebuild Your Audience From Day 1

Even with no money, you can grow a brand if you show up daily.

Use these 3 free tools:

Email list (Mailerlite or ConvertKit free tier)

Facebook group or Instagram account

Google My Business if local

From your brand materials:

"People don't remember products. They remember people. Build your personal brand like you're running for office."

Stat: 92% of consumers trust recommendations from individuals over companies—especially when buying from small businesses (Source: Nielsen).

Post results. Share customer wins. Tell stories. Be real and consistent.

7. Work Like You've Got a Deadline—Because You Do

You don't have time to play small. You don't need more learning. You need more doing.

From Making the Leap Full-Time:

"Don't fool yourself with busy work. Sitting at the computer doesn't usually make people money. Getting in front of people or getting on the phone is what makes money."
-Eric F Gilbert

If you had to rebuild:

Wake up at 6 a.m.

Message 20 new prospects before 9 a.m.

Create content by noon

Fulfill and serve clients until 6 p.m.

Track every sale, every lead, every conversion

This isn't forever—but it is necessary right now.

Starting over doesn't mean starting from scratch.
It means starting from experience.

If you had to rebuild tomorrow:

You'd skip the fluff

You'd start with what works

You'd move with urgency

You'd protect your time

And you'd sell something that solves a real
problem from day one

This is the blueprint to restart fast, grow lean,
and build better.

Now go build it like you mean it.

8. Your Network Shapes Your Net Worth

"You are the average of the five people you spend the most time with."

— Jim Rohn

This principle underscores the significant influence your close associations have on your mindset, habits, and ultimately, your success.

Why does this matter? Because your environment can either propel you forward or hold you back. Surrounding yourself with individuals who are ambitious, financially savvy, and growth-oriented can inspire and challenge you to elevate your own standards. Conversely, spending time with those who are complacent or negative can impede your progress.

Stat: According to research, individuals tend to mirror the behaviors and attitudes of their closest peers, affecting their financial decisions and overall success.

9. The "Five Monkeys Experiment": A Lesson in Conformity

Consider the allegorical "Five Monkeys Experiment," which illustrates how group behavior can perpetuate outdated or unproductive practices:

Five monkeys are placed in a cage with a ladder leading to bananas. When one monkey climbs the ladder, all are sprayed with cold water.

Eventually, the monkeys prevent any from climbing the ladder to avoid the spray.

One by one, monkeys are replaced with new ones who, despite never experiencing the spray, continue the behavior because "that's how it's always been done."

While the literal experiment's authenticity is debated, it serves as a powerful metaphor for how societal norms and peer pressure can discourage innovation and maintain the status quo.

10. Choose Your Circle Wisely

Your social circle can either:

Lift you up: Successful individuals often support and mentor others, sharing knowledge and opportunities.

Hold you back: Those who are envious or fearful may discourage your ambitions, consciously or unconsciously.

Stat: Studies suggest that individuals are significantly influenced by their social networks, affecting behaviors ranging from health habits to financial decisions.

Action Steps:

Audit your circle: Reflect on whether your close contacts inspire growth or foster stagnation.

Seek mentorship: Engage with those who have achieved what you aspire to; their insights can be invaluable.

Limit negativity: Reduce time spent with individuals who consistently undermine your goals or exhibit toxic behaviors.

Final Thought:

If you aim to rebuild or elevate your life and business, start by evaluating and, if necessary, reshaping your environment. Surround yourself with those who reflect the success and values you strive for. Remember, your trajectory is not just determined by your efforts but also by the company you keep.

Chapter 16: Resources & Templates

Practical Tools to Help You Start, Run, and Scale
Like a Business Boss

"Success is not just about knowing what to do—it's about having the tools to do it."

**— Adapted from The E-Myth Revisited,
Michael Gerber**

You've learned the mindset, strategy, and structure needed to build a profitable business. Now it's time to equip yourself with resources and templates that make implementation faster, more efficient, and more effective.

1. Legal & Formation Tools

Business Registration
Be sure to check out the package that we offer!

Sunbiz.org (Florida LLC/S-Corp formation)

IRS.gov (Free EIN number for all U.S. businesses)

ZenBusiness or Incfile – Budget-friendly business registration services (LLC, S-Corp, EIN, Operating Agreements)

Document Templates
You can search for many of these online for free, but keep them in your Google Drive for easy access!

Operating Agreement (for LLCs)

Independent Contractor Agreement

Service Terms & Conditions (client onboarding)

Stat: Businesses with proper legal setup are more likely to qualify for credit, grants, and vendor contracts (Source: U.S. Small Business Administration).

2. Financial & Tax Tools

Banking & Accounting

Novo or Bluevine (online business banking)

QuickBooks Online or Wave Accounting (bookkeeping, invoicing)

Gusto (payroll if you hire employees or pay yourself as an S-Corp)

Tracking Templates

Monthly Profit & Loss Tracker (Google Sheet)

Client Payment Tracker (Google Sheet)

Tax Deduction Worksheet

Stat: 82% of small businesses fail due to poor cash flow management—not lack of sales (U.S. Bank study).

3. Sales & Marketing Tools

CRM and Lead Tracking

HubSpot CRM (free tier available)

Pipedrive (visual sales pipeline)

Notion or Trello (custom lead tracking boards)

Website & Funnel Builders
(remember Chat GPT can write your html for this)

Carrd or Squarespace (fast, simple websites)

ClickFunnels or Systeme.io (for building sales funnels)

WordPress (for advanced content marketing/blog SEO)

Email Marketing

MailerLite or ConvertKit (automation, landing pages, email sequences)

Templates

Sales Call Script Template
Chat GPT can help you script these. Just remember to use pain points, not features.

DM Outreach Script (short-form for Instagram/LinkedIn)

Client Onboarding Email Template

"Thank You for Booking" Email

4. Content & Branding Tools

Design

Canva (free and Pro versions for content, proposals, social graphics)

Looka or LogoMakr (logo design for startups)

Scheduling & Posting

Meta Business Suite (for Facebook/Instagram)

Later or Buffer (social media scheduling across platforms)

Content Templates

30-Day Social Media Calendar (pre-filled with prompts)

Content Repurposing Grid (turn one post into five)

Authority Builder Worksheet (track client wins, testimonials, before/after results)

Stat: Businesses that post consistently on social media generate 23% more revenue on average than those that don't (Source: Sprout Social).

5. Productivity & Automation Tools

Scheduling & Time Management

Calendly or Acuity (client booking and calendar sync)

Google Calendar + Color-coded time blocking

Notion or ClickUp (workflow tracking)

Automation

Zapier (connects apps to automate repetitive tasks)

Loom (record SOPs and client walkthroughs)

ChatGPT (content ideation, draft writing, client email scripts)

Templates

Weekly CEO Time Block Template

Daily "Big 3" Priority Sheet

Real-Time Weekly Time Audit Worksheet (from Chapter 11)

6. Client Success & Retention Tools

Feedback & Testimonials

Google Forms or Typeform (collect testimonials)

Post-job email templates to request Google Reviews

"Client Win" form (capture before/after transformations)

Client Portal

Notion client dashboard (share updates, links, resources)

Trello board for onboarding and progress tracking

Retention Templates

219

Monthly Check-In Email

Referral Rewards Program Terms

Anniversary or Thank You Email Template

Stat: Repeat customers spend 67% more than new customers (Source: Bain & Company).

7. Business Planning Templates

Planning Docs

One-Page Business Plan (Google Doc)

Quarterly Goals & KPIs Sheet

Cash Flow Forecast Template

Vision Statement & Core Values Template

Quote:

"A goal without a plan is just a wish."

— Antoine de Saint-Exupéry

These templates make it easier to work on your business instead of just grinding away inside it.

Business Boss Templates

Client Payment Tracker

Client Name | Service/Product | Invoice Date | Amount | Paid? (Y/N) | Payment Method | Notes
------------|------------------|--------------|--------|------
-------|----------------|-------
John Smith | Logo Design | 4/1/2025 | $550 | Y | Stripe | —
Jane Doe | LLC Formation | 4/3/2025 | $550 | N | PayPal | Sent reminder

Monthly Profit & Loss Tracker

Category	Income	Expenses	Notes
Services Sold	$3,000	—	
Product Sales	$1,200	—	
Advertising	—	$300	Google Ads
Software	—	$75	Canva + Calendly
Profit (auto)	$4,200	$375	=Income - Expenses

Real-Time Time Audit Worksheet

Time Slot | Task Performed | Category
| High/Low Payoff?
--------------|----------------------------|------------------
|------------------
8:00–8:15 AM | Checked emails | Admin
| Low
8:15–8:30 AM | Sent invoices | Admin
| Low
8:30–8:45 AM | Followed up with lead | Sales
| High
8:45–9:00 AM | Watched YouTube video |
Distraction | Low

DM Outreach Script

Hey [Name], I love what you're doing in [industry/business]. Quick question:
Do you need help with [result your offer provides]?
I help [who] get [outcome] without [pain point]. Let me know if I can send over a quick breakdown. No pressure!

Sales Call Script

Opening:
"Hey [Name], I'm excited to learn more about your business. I'd love to ask a few questions to see where you're at and how I might be able to help."

Key Questions:
- What's the biggest challenge you're facing right now?
- What have you tried already?
- What result would make this worth it for you?

Close:
"Based on what you've told me, I believe [Your Offer] would be a great fit. Here's what it looks like…"

Price Presentation:
"It's [$X] for [result]. You'll have [X weeks of support/delivery] and everything we discussed is included."

Final Question:
"Would you like to move forward or have any questions before we get started?"

Thank You for Booking Email

Subject: You're In! Here's What Happens Next

Hi [Client Name],

Thanks so much for booking [Service Name]. I'm excited to get started.

Here's what to expect next:
- [Outline next step #1]
- [Outline next step #2]
- [Attach any docs, links, or instructions]

Your scheduled session is confirmed for:
[Date and Time]

If you have any questions before we begin, just reply to this email.

Talk soon,
[Your Name]

One-Page Business Plan

Business Name:
Founder:
Mission Statement: What problem do you solve
and for whom?

Offer:
What do you sell? Be specific.

Target Market:
Who are your ideal clients?

Marketing Strategy:
How will people find you?

Revenue Model:
How will you make money?

Launch Plan:
What are the next 5 actions you'll take to
launch/grow?

Referral Program Terms

Refer a Friend – Get Rewarded!
Know someone who could use [Service/Product Name]?

Here's how it works:
- Refer them by sharing this link: [Your Link]
- They book and pay? You get [Reward: $50 cash, free month, etc.]
- Unlimited referrals. No expiration.

Thank you for helping us grow!

30-Day Social Media Calendar (Sample)

```
Day | Content Type    | Topic Example
----|-----------------|------------------------------
1  | Personal Story  | Why I started my business
2  | Testimonial     | Screenshot or quote from a
happy client
3  | Tip/How-To      | 3 things to avoid when
starting an LLC
4  | FAQ             | "Do I need a separate bank
account?"
5  | Value Post      | Explain EIN vs. SSN
```

Final Word: Tools Don't Replace Hustle—They Multiply It

Having the right templates and tech won't build your business for you—but they can dramatically reduce friction and help you focus where it matters most: on growth, results, and freedom.

Use these tools to:

Stay organized

Look professional

Deliver consistent value

Scale faster without burning out

Your future business is built with what you do today. Make every move count.

Would you like me to format all chapters into a Google Doc now for export or Kindle upload? Or do you want to write the Acknowledgments and About the Author section next?

Here are the Acknowledgments and About the Author sections, written in a clean, professional, and direct tone that matches the rest of your book.

Acknowledgments

No business owner reaches success alone—and neither does any author.

First, thank you to every client who trusted me, challenged me, and pushed me to think bigger. Your questions, struggles, and breakthroughs shaped the content of this book. This is your blueprint as much as it is mine.

To the small business owners who wake up early, stay up late, and never stop trying—you're the heartbeat of the economy. You don't get the headlines, but you create the jobs, build the communities, and prove that hustle and heart still matter.

To the entrepreneurs who read this book in the middle of the night because quitting isn't an option—keep going. There's more ahead for you than behind you.

Sources and References

Books by the Author

- Gilbert, Eric. *LLC or S-Corp? Making the Right Move for Your Business*.

- Gilbert, Eric. *How to Day Trade Without Losing Your Shirt (And Stay Legal Doing It)*.

- Additional unpublished material and blog content authored by Eric Gilbert, used with permission.

Websites and Business Tools

- VizzyBrand.com – Marketing strategies, corporate setup guidance, and small business growth content

- GetStockTips.com – Day trading tactics and stock selection principles

- TheJamaicaBrand.com – Brand extension strategy, ecommerce, and client retention methods

- FishingEric.com – Content on brand merchandising and niche product marketing

- Sunbiz.org – Florida Division of Corporations

- SCORE.org – Free small business mentoring and tools

- TradingView.com – Trading and market analysis platform

- Canva.com – Design tool for entrepreneurs

- Fiverr.com – Freelance services marketplace

Books by Other Authors

- Kiyosaki, Robert. *Rich Dad Poor Dad*. Warner Books, 1997.

- Gerber, Michael E. *The E-Myth Revisited: Why Most Small Businesses Don't Work and What to Do About It*. Harper Business, 1995.

- Sinek, Simon. *Start with Why: How Great Leaders Inspire Everyone to Take Action*. Portfolio, 2009.

- Byrne, Rhonda. *The Secret*. Atria Books, 2006.

- Olson, Jeff. *The Slight Edge: Turning Simple Disciplines into Massive Success and Happiness*. Greenleaf Book Group Press, 2013.

- Hill, Napoleon. *Think and Grow Rich*. The Ralston Society, 1937.

Notable Entrepreneurs Referenced

- Warren Buffett – Concepts and philosophy sourced from public interviews, *Berkshire Hathaway Annual Letters*, and *The Snowball: Warren Buffett and the Business of Life* by Alice Schroeder.

- Oprah Winfrey – Background and insights based on public speeches and works such as *The Life You Want*.

- Dave Sandler – Sales principles drawn from *The Sandler Rules* by David Mattson and Sandler Training resources.

- Daymond John – Branding and growth strategy referenced from *The Power of Broke* and *Rise and Grind*.

- Howard Schultz – Strategy and leadership insights taken from *Pour Your Heart Into It* and *Onward*.

Studies, Quotes, and Data

- "You are the average of the five people you spend the most time with." – Attributed to Jim Rohn.

- Monkey/Ladder/Banana Experiment – Commonly referenced in organizational psychology; anecdotal origin with no peer-reviewed source.

- U.S. Small Business Administration (SBA) – Statistics on startup success and failure.

- U.S. Census Bureau – Data on income distribution and self-employment rates.

- Bureau of Labor Statistics – Labor market trends and entrepreneurship data.

- Harvard Business Review – Research on team performance, funding strategies, and scaling.

- Forbes and Entrepreneur.com – Business development, marketing, and branding strategies.

Special thanks to my wife for being my partner in life and in business. Your drive, vision, and faith inspire me every day.

And finally, to every mentor, coach, and teacher who showed me that business isn't about luck— it's about doing the work, making smart decisions, and refusing to settle.

Thank you.

Scan to order

www.ingramcontent.com/pod-product-compliance
Lightning Source LLC
Chambersburg PA
CBHW031847200326
41597CB00012B/299